BOURNVILLE

A Portrait of Cadbury's Garden Village in Old Picture Postcards

by
Edwin Gumbley

S.B. Publications
1991

This Book is Dedicated to the Memory of
OLWYN NICOLLE
31st December 1949 to 7th March 1990
A teacher at Bournville Junior School from 1972 to 1984
A close family friend for over twenty years

First published by S.B. Publications

Unit 2, The Old Station Yard, Pipe Gate, Market Drayton, Shropshire, TF9 4HY

ISBN 1.870708.69.5

Typeset, printed and bound by Manchester Free Press, Paragon Mill, Jersey Street, Manchester M4 6FP

CONTENTS

BOURNVILLE SCHOOLS, WOODBROOKE ROAD, THORN ROAD, BOURNVILLE PARK AND BEECH ROAD

THE MENS' RECREATION GROUND AND FACTORY

THE GREEN, BOURNVILLE

MAPLE ROAD TO SYCAMORE ROAD, INCLUDING HOLLY GROVE

MISCELLANEOUS

S.B. Publications

BIBLIOGRAPHY

Peter Atkins; *The Architecture of Bournville 1879/1914*
Barbara Tilson (ed); *Made in Birmingham, Design and Industry 1889-1989,* Brewin Books, 1989.
A.G. Gardner, *Life of George Cadbury,* London, Cassell & Co, 1923.
I.A. Williams, *The Firm of Cadbury 1831-1931,* London, Constable & Co, 1931.
The Bournville Village Trust 1900-1955. A Bournville Village Trust Publication, 1956.
Kelly's Directories 1895 to 1935.
Additional Reading:
The history of Bournville is well documented, most books on Birmingham will have a chapter on the Cadbury's or Bournville and often both.

ACKNOWLEDGEMENTS

All the postcard dealers and collectors who have either saved or sent me Bournville post cards over the years, and especially the well-known 'dealer' who barked ''nobody collects Bournville postcards it's worse than collecting postcards of Enfield!''.

Edited by Steve Benz.

THE AUTHOR

Edwin Gumbley grew up in Bournville in the 1960s and has sentimental memories of a place with no public houses, no fish and chip shops, a newsagent that did not even open on a Sunday and 'locals' who complained about too much traffic; he now lives in relaxed obscurity in Barnt Green, Worcestershire. Many older Bournville residents will remember his aunt, Hilda Gumbley, associated for many years with the annual pantomime in the Concert Hall and maypole dancing at the Childrens' Festival every June.

INTRODUCTION
The Cadbury Brothers and Bournville Village

Two words often come to mind when you mention chocolate — Cadbury and Bournville; add to this picture postcards of 'The Factory in a Garden' from earlier this century and you have this book.

The story starts in 1879 when the two Cadbury brothers, Richard and George (their grandfather having moved to Birmingham in 1794) decided to move their expanding cocoa and chocolate business from premises in Bridge Street, Birmingham. Having outgrown that factory, they were keen as manufacturers of food products to move out of the polluted atmosphere of central Birmingham.

The brothers chose an area four-and-a-half miles away, known locally as Bournbrook; a shallow valley with a brook and at its eastern end, a single track railway and a canal. The brothers, who were never slow to seize a commercial opportunity, decided to change the name of the location of their new factory to Bournville; adding a French edge and with it the implication of fashionable exclusivity and quality.

Initially, the factory and sixteen houses for key workers were built on fourteen acres next to the railway. Each house set in one sixth of an acre of land. All the other employees had to be brought to work from Birmingham by train or walked over fields from the hamlets of Stirchley, Cotteridge or Selly Oak. Once the factory was well established, around 1890, George Cadbury began to devote some of his spare time to provide housing for working families. His first venture was a group of cottages one-and-a-half miles away in Northfield. The success of the 'Bournville Works' enabled the Brothers to buy land around the factory; an example being the twenty-four acres bought from the Martin family in 1893 to create the Girls' and Mens' Recreation Grounds.

Shortly after this, George Cadbury began to buy more land adjacent to the factory. By 1895 the first houses were being built in Bournville at Linden Road (on the apex of the hill), Selly Oak Road (Row Heath Lane at the time), and the western end of Maryvale Road.

By late 1900, the Estate had grown to 313 houses on 330 acres and George Cadbury decided to establish the Bournville Village Trust. The formation of the Trust enabled George Cadbury to surrender all his private interest in both the capital and revenue of the Estate. The Trust was the creation of George Cadbury, not the firm of Cadbury, and its existence has always been separate. Equally, at no time in the history of Bournville Village Trust has more than forty per cent of the residents of the Estate been employed by Cadbury's.

Richard Cadbury built the Almshouses on the corner of Maryvale and Linden Roads in 1898, and the 38 houses adjoining which provided rents for their upkeep; this was a separate development to the houses being built by George Cadbury and subsequently the Bournville Village Trust.

Some of the postcards in this book have been postally used, others not. All of them have been bought over the past few years and form about twenty-five per cent of my collection. In the not too distant past when access to the telephone was not as easy as it is today postcards provided a means of sending messages — some important, a few funny, most mundane. At the time of posting the sender would have thought of no better way to convey their message than a view of Bournville, Cadbury's "Factory in a Garden".

Edwin Gumbley
February 1991

GEORGE CADBURY
(19th September 1839 — 24th October 1922) Founder of the Bournville Village Trust, captitalist, philanthropist and social reformer.

THE LIBRARY

George Cadbury contributed £3,000 towards the building of the public library in Bournville Lane, Stirchley; a small village lying to the east of Bournville. Posted on the 29th December 1908, the postcard told the receiver that it was bitterly cold and had been snowing nearly all day.

BOURNVILLE LANE

The bridge carries the Birmingham to Worcester Canal and the Midland Railway which had taken over the Birmingham Western and Suburban line by 1884. Arthur James Dewey was the Station Master from 1900 to 1929. Posted 29th September 1908 with the message: ''Just to wish you many Happy Returns''.

BOURNVILLE LANE. BOURNVILLE.

BOURNVILLE LANE

Posted 30th July 1927, the message reads: ''Having a lovely time, we went over the works on Monday, it was very interesting indeed''.

BOURNVILLE LANE

The houses in the background are the original ones built by George Gadd to house key workers close to the Cadbury factory in 1879. Some were demolished in 1914, the site is now occupied by the Dining Block of the Cadbury factory site.

CLUB AND GIRLS' BATH

Built in 1905, the girls' swimming bath is 24 by 14 metres with a capacity of 477,000 litres. Internally it had 87 cubicals and 27 spray showers. Many thousands of women have learnt to swim here as it was company policy to allow them to learn during work time.

DINING R'MS & RECREATION BLOCK. BOURNVILLE WORKS

DINING ROOMS AND RECREATION BLOCK

The Dining and Recreation block was completed in 1927 and designed by James Millar of Glasgow. The ground slopes away from the road, giving the building two storeys at the front and three at the rear. The building measures 83 metres by 61 metres.

BOURNVILLE LANE

This was taken during the Cadbury Centenary Celebrations of 1931. The Dining Block in the rear had 12 dining rooms of various sizes for workers, clerks, foremen, forewomen, staffs A & B and directors. The oak footbridge on the right connected the Girls and Mens Grounds.

BOURNVILLE LANE

This view shows the rustic country feel to Bournville Lane. Its original name had been Oak Lane.
The card was never posted, it is almost certainly pre-1914.

BOURNVILLE LANE.

BOURNBROOK HALL

A corner of Bournville Hall can be seen on the right; its original name being Bournbrook Hall. By October 1879 the whole area around had changed its name to Bournville to assume certain French pretensions prevalent at the time.

The Wrench Series No. 8383

BOURNBROOK HALL

In 1893 the Cadbury Brothers bought the Martin family estate, including this old Georgian House, along with 24 acres of meadows and parklands to create the recreation grounds for the male and female employees.

THE SIGNAL STATION

The Signal Station was located on the south-west corner of the Mens Recreation Ground at the junction of Bournville Lane and Linden Road. Posted 20th May 1915, the message reads: ''I have not been ill, it was the rain that stopped me coming to town on Wednesday''.

The Flagstaff. Bournville

BOURNVILLE LANE

This house stands on the corner of Beech Road and Bournville Lane looking down towards Linden Road. The photographer was O.W. (Octavious William) Evans who owned the chemist shop on Bournville Green from 1907. He nearly always prefixed the numbering of his postcards with an E; a number of examples of his work are shown in this book.

BOURNVILLE LANE

These houses were built in the late 1890s. Notice the steep roof, with the bedroom window frame taken into the roof to reduce the use of costly bricks. Architects George Punshon and Francis Andrews were responsible for a number of the blocks of houses on Bournville Lane.

BOURNVILLE LANE

Prior to the house numbering in 1907 in this part of Bournville Lane, the houses had names such as Lamorna Cottage, Bigbury and Rhodesia. The black and white house in the background is the Lodge and Washing Baths in Laurel Grove, designed by W A Harvey in 1896.

SELLY OAK ROAD

Selly Oak Road is one of the older Bournville Roads and was originally called Row Heath Lane. Probably a 1920s postcard, and photographed prior to the continuation to Bournville Lane being cut through to the Bristol Road.

E.23. BOURNVILLE. MARYVALE ROAD.

MARYVALE ROAD

In 1895 the first houses were built on the north side of Maryvale Road; on the ridge which is the southern line of what was Bournville. A number of these houses were designed by Alfred Walker who later worked as a surveyor on the Bournville Estate.

MARYVALE ROAD

The majority of the houses built in Bournville before 1903 were designed by William Alexander Harvey (1875-1951). They often had interesting styling points; here the white painted rough cast and corner buttresses were influenced by the architect Charles Voysey (1857-1941). These designs can also be found in Holly Grove.

MARY VALE RD.   BOURVILLE

MARYVALE ROAD

The first shops on Bournville were built in 1897, on the corner of Maryvale and Linden Road. The occupants in 1904 were D. Roy (baker) who moved down to Bournville Green in 1907, Misses C. & A. Kelland (fancy drapers), and finally on the corner H.W. Smith (grocer).

MARYVALE ROAD

In 1898 Richard Cadbury had 38 houses built on the upper eastern side of Linden Road and the north side of Maryvale Road to provide funds for the running of the Almshouses. The delivery cart in the picture belonged to Ralph Witherford, family butcher, 134 Pershore Road, Cotteridge. He began trading in 1908 and was still there in 1928.

THE ALMSHOUSES

Richard Cadbury never lived to see the first tenants take up residence in the Almshouses. He died of diphtheria in March 1899 while on holiday with his family in Jerusalem.

THE QUADRANGLE, THE ALMSHOUSES

The Almshouses are grouped to form a low-level single storied quadrangle centred around a clock tower. Initially, an orchard belonging to Bournbrook Hall was reserved for the residents at the rear.

202 ALMSHOUSES BOURNEVILLE

THE ALMSHOUSES

The thirty-three almshouses were originally intended for each dwelling to accommodate two people who had reached the age of sixty. They consisted of a living room, a curtained-off bedroom and a small kitchen. They have since been refurbished to modern standards.

BOURNEVILLE - PART OF GIRL'S RECREATION GROUNDS

THE GIRLS' RECREATION GROUNDS

In 1896 the grounds of Bournbrook Hall, about twelve acres, were made into the Girls' Recreation Grounds. Latterly it had been known as Bournville Hall Home for Girls; the Matron at the time Emma W Rayner. The Hall was demolished in 1907.

THE GIRLS' RECREATION GROUND

The Girls' Recreation Ground had a gymnasium, hockey pitch and netball and tennis courts, although it was less formerly set out than the Mens' Recreation Ground. A large part of the grounds was laid out as gardens and lawns.

LINDEN ROAD

In 1893 George Cadbury bought 120 acres of land around the factory and began building within two years. The new 'Village' had as it most northerly point the junction of Linden Road and Oak Tree Lane.

LINDEN ROAD

After 1903 A W Harvey was no longer the Trust's architect, having left for private practice. The design of houses became more simple and were built mainly in blocks of two, with a few blocks of three and four.

LINDEN ROAD

Linden Road follows the former 'Drive' leading up to Bournbrook Hall. The houses at the top of the hill on the right were built circa 1896. Before the numbering of this part of the road after 1906, they had flamboyant names like Gripeswyke Cottage, Aufenthalt and Nashville House.

LINDEN ROAD

One of the re-occurring features of the houses in early Bournville was their simple design, with variations of theme which included bay windows giving three sources of light and mullions to give the impression of variety and lack of dull conformity.

LINDEN ROAD
The simple and practical cottage style of this block of three houses gives the impression it might be bigger than it really is. The garden is 6 metres at the front and 30 metres at the rear.

RUSKIN HALL

Ruskin Hall was built in 1903 as a social centre for Bournville Estate. It was established as a School of Crafts in 1911 when the City of Birmingham absorbed Bournville from Worcestershire along with Kings Norton and Northfield U.D.C.

LINDEN ROAD

The house on the left side of this semi-detached block was sold by the Trustees to become a Vicarage, the Bournville Village Trust giving £400 towards its costs.

THE FRIENDS MEETING HOUSE

The Meeting House contains a mixture of architectural styles - Tudor window, Roman door and curlique guttering supports - designed by A W Harvey who also designed Ruskin Hall. Richard and George Cadbury built a number of Friends Meeting Houses over the years in Cotteridge, Stirchley, Northfield, Selly Oak and Hay Green; this building was to be the last.

THE FRIENDS MEETING HOUSE
The original plan for the Meeting House was to build a much smaller building. George Cadbury followed the advice of the builder to demolish a back wall already two metres high and extend the building at the rear by over a third.

THE CHURCH HALL
The Church Hall was built in 1912 by public subscription on land that was given by the Bournville Village Trust. Posted on 3rd September 1913, the postcard reads: "This is a lovely place. Arrived quite safe".

PARISH CHURCH . BOURNVILLE.

THE PARISH CHURCH

The Church Hall was used for services until the parish Church of St. Francis, designed in a Lombardic style by the architect W A Harvey, was built in 1925. Inside it has some good modern carving mainly by John Poole. They are now linked by cloisters built in 1937.

LINDEN ROAD

Looking up past the cross road with Bournville Lane to the south ridge behind the now demolished Bournbrook Hall, and to Maryvale Road. Just to the right of this picture was the original Bournville Post Office, which subsequently moved to the Green in 1907.

LINDEN ROAD

Before these houses were built in the late 1890s, the land was used by men from the factory as a make shift football pitch; prior to the Mens' Recreation Grounds being opened.

THE OLD FARM INN

Originally known as Froggatt's Farm, an ancient building which is now hardly recognizable as part of the Old Farm Inn. At this time it was a Coffee House owned by Mrs Marie Bodycote who carried on the business following the death of her husband John in 1901.

LINDEN ROAD

Ewen Harper was the architect for the Linden Road and Maryvale Road houses, including the Almshouses. The rents from the houses paid for the upkeep and running of the Almshouses.

MARYVALE ROAD
Another view of the first shops to be built in Bournville. An image of market town construction, with the architect R.N. Shaw's influence (Bedford Park, West London 1880) half-timbered upper floors and the use of rough cast and small leaded windows — to be repeated again for one side of Bournville Green some years later.

The Schools, Bournville, near Birmingham
(Covered with Precelly Rustic Slates)

JV 54789

BOURNVILLE SCHOOLS

This is a product order card sent by a manufacturer on receipt of an order by a customer. The reverse reads: "The Precelly Rustic Slates — STRONG DURABLE, QUAINT, ARTISTIC - Portmadoc....191 ..Your.....of.....is duly to hand, and will have our careful attention. Yours truly, DAVISS BROS."

BOURNVILLE SCHOOL
The hall of the school has mural decorations depicting Biblical scenes, painted in 1914 by Mary Sargent Florence and Mary Chreighton McDowall. The plan for the school was that generally used for schools at the time; the classrooms opening off the main assembly hall.

BOURNVILLE SCHOOL

George Cadbury gave two-and a half acres of land for the Bournville Village School to be built in 1905; a mixed primary school accommodating initially 540 pupils. The ultimate cost to George Cadbury excluding the land was £30,000.

BOURNVILLE INFANTS' SCHOOL

Photographed on 22nd January 1910 and showing Ursula Cadbury laying the foundation stone for Bournville Infants School, with parents George, Elizabeth and her sisters Eleanor and Isobel. The builder William Bishop and architect William Alexander Harvey are to the right of the group.

BOURNVILLE INFANTS' SCHOOL

Postally used on 5th September 1915, the postcard was sent from Welshpool to Halifax, Yorkshire. One tends to think that the four youngsters have been excused from class for the picture, as a figure can be seen 'hovering' to the left and a girl can be seen on the steps of the primary school.

BOURNVILLE INFANTS' SCHOOL
Published by O W Evans and probably dated pre-1915. The hedge in the foreground still being
very young and similar to the dated picture illustrated on page 45.

BOURNVILLE SCHOOL

George and Elizabeth Cadbury had the carillion built in the school tower after being impressed by the one in Bruges, Belgium. It had a set of twenty-two bells and was housed in the stone belfry, on the north-west angle of the tower.

THE CARILLION

The carillion was modernised in 1934 and the number of bells expanded to forty eight. This shows the frame of several tiers during its manufacture, in which the bells hang fixed; the largest being over 3 tons.

BOURNVILLE SCHOOL

A view of the school tower and cupola following its modernisation in 1934. The cupola was designed by the architect of the school, W A Harvey. The photograph was taken by Albert Creed, tobacconist, Bournville Green from 1928.

WOODBROOKE ROAD

Maps of Bournville dated 1899, show Thorn and Woodbrook Road as one (not unlike a dog's hind leg) leading from Bournville Park to Linden Road, then continuing across to Hazel Road and down to Sycamore Road.

WOODBROOKE ROAD

These houses were built around 1907. Again the simple cottage design with the added variety of white rough cast above the bedroom windows. Henry Bedford Tylor was now the Bournville Trust architect, his houses were plainer and more modest than those designed by Harvey.

WOODBROOKE ROAD

These two groups of bungalows for occupation by elderly people were built in 1909. Posted on 10th January 1915, the postcard reads: "The end bungalow on the right near the little tree is Miss Davies".

WOODBROOKE ROAD

The second group of bungalows on Woodbrooke Road and photographed receiving its daily delivery of milk. The flagpole at the rear belonged to Fircroft Working Men's College.

WOODBROOKE ROAD
Looking back from Oak Tree Lane towards the Bournville Schools. Posted on 17th August 1911
the postcard reads: ''I hope you are all going on alright. I am enjoying myself champion''.

Published by
A.D.Co.
48.Bristol.Street.

Thorne Road.(Showing Beach Road) Bournville.

THORN ROAD

The author grew up in this road. The houses were built in 1908-09, apart from some of those on the
left, dating from around 1904. The later houses were designed by H B Tyler who died in 1915.
Posted on 9th January 1913 it reads: ''Parcel received this morning, many thanks''.

FLOOD IN BOURNVILLE PARK

The author's father would have been 14 months old and no doubt wrapped up warmly in his parents new house in Thorn Road when this flood took place in May 1908.

BOURNVILLE PARK

The 7-acre Bournville Park was laid out in 1907 and transferred to the City of Birmingham in 1920. The Park provides a link between the Cadbury factory and the Village Green to the Hay Green area; it also links up with the Valley Park Way.

BEECH ROAD
Most of Beech Road was designed in 1897. The blocks, bottom right before the Park and top left
(out of view), were built a little later.

BEECH ROAD, BOURNVILLE.

BEECH ROAD

Once again at the top of Beech Road and looking down towards the Park and Thorn Road. By following the line of the road, one is able to see its curve prior to the extension of Woodbrook Road to the west. Though not dated this is an early type of photographic card by McCaw, Stevenson & Orr Ltd, circa 1903.

THE MENS' RECREATION GROUND
The Mens' Recreation Ground was laid in 1896 with one football pitch, two hockey grounds, two cricket pitches, three lawn tennis courts and two bowling greens. Later, hard tennis courts and an open-air swimming bath were added. The original key worker houses can be seen on left.

THE MENS' RECREATION GROUND
In the earlier part of this century the cricket pitch was regarded as one of the best in the Midlands, producing a number of well-known cricketers of the day; Arthur Lilley of Warwickshire and J B Higgins who captained Worcestershire.

THE PAVILLION

The Pavillion was built in 1902 by Cadbury's and given to the male employees in commemoration of the coronation of Edward VII. The Pavillion provided accommodation, changing rooms and was equipped with showers and a gymnasium.

WORKS SUMMER PARTY, 1906

From the opening of the Pavillion on 18th June 1902 until 1906, The Works Summer Party was held on the Mens' Grounds. No 'Party' was held in 1907 due to the death of Mrs Richard Cadbury. It was then transferred to the Girls Grounds until 1914. Following the first world war, the company became too big to hold such a party. The postcard possibly illustrates one of the Summer Parties held before 1906.

THE PAVILLION

The figure sitting to the left of the clock face is George Cadbury; the event again is unknown. It is all male, with men in working clothes. George Cadbury and his son, George junior had a life-long interest in the Male Adult School Movement; it is possible this is such a meeting.

"SIXTY YEARS OF BOURNVILLE COCOA"

An event to celebrate sixty years of Bournville cocoa in 1913. Playing on an historical theme it showed how female dress had changed over the period, but not Bournville cocoa which was not strictly true. The real growth of Cadbury's in the late 19th century was based on cocoa essence which was not produced until late in 1866 and Bournville cocoa did not arrive until 1906. (This is one of a series of 6 cards).

THE "BIRD BATH" AND TERRACE

The Dining Room Block which overlooks the Mens' Recreation Ground was partly erected after the first world war and completed in 1927. The basement provided changing rooms for 5,000 'girls', with youth club rooms on the upper floors, a library, doctors' and dentists' surgeries. On the other side of the building is a Concert Hall seating 1,050 people.

THE "NEW" COCOA BLOCK

The 'new' Cocoa Block was completed in 1929 on the site of the 'old' saw mill which was transferred to Blackpole, Worcestershire. Posted 3rd April 1936, the message reads: "I am just sending you a card of Cadbury's works. I will not be home to go to Gilwern, so tell Mr Davies I will not be there".

BOURNVILLE WORKS

At its opening the Cocoa Block was at the 'cutting edge' of the mechanical technology of the day. By gravity feed from the upper floors, the cocoa, tin canisters and paper lining bags were brought together, weighed & labelled for despatch on the ground floor. A view from Bournville School tower.

GENERAL OFFICE

Upon moving to Bournville in 1879, the General Office consisted of eight people. By 1920 it had grown to around two hundred and fifty staff, dealing with a million separate orders per year. Notice the male figure on the roof. This building is one of earliest in the factory.

BOURNVILLE WORKS AND STATION
In 1879 the railway running through Bournville was a single track branch line approaching Birmingham from the south-west terminating at Granville Street. In the 1880s it was converted to double track and extended to New Street, Birmingham.

VIEW FROM SCHOOL TOWER, BOURNVILLE
Pritchard Series postcards were published between 1917 and 1919 by Florence Pritchard, newsagent, 253 Maryvale Road, Bournville. The picture is a copy of an Adco postcard of 1914 and shows what the Bournville Works looked like before the first world war.

CADBURY'S WORKS FROM THE RAILWAY STATION
The railway track in the picture was laid in 1884 and connected the external track to the then Stockroom. Prior to this, goods were transported by horse and cart to Lifford Station. This loading area was superceded in 1908 by the new Stockroom, built a little to the north. The picture is dated c.1912.

CARD BOX AND PRINTING DEPARTMENT

Q Block was a single-storey building measuring 180 by 61 metres wide. It was extended three times, and was demolished in the early 1980s. It consisted of three departments: printing, card cutting, and card box making, with a central raised gangway.

BOURNVILLE WORKS

Q Block can be seen stretching away from the CADBURY BOURNVILLE lettering in the right foreground. The Dining Block is visible but not the Cocoa Block, dating the card to around 1927. The works covered 81 acres and the recreation grounds a further 110 acres. Within a few years of this picture, the factory floor space was 38 acres, with 2 miles of road and 5 miles of railway track.

Bourneville-
Girls Entering Works.

GIRLS ENTERING WORKS

Women have played a pivitol role in the growth of Cadbury's. Apart from a slight drop in the
female members of the workforce in 1893, there was an uninterrupted growth in their number;
men only out numbering them in 1919.

GIRLS AT WORK (BOX-MAKING)
Six to seven hundred females were taken on every year, while some hundreds left due to marriage
and other causes. Posted 10th January 1908, the postcard reads: ''Thank you for your postcard, I
hope you like this''.

GIRLS IN DINING ROOM

Save for a few cleaners who put in an hour or two a day, no married women were employed at Bournville; this fitted into the social norms of the time. Posted 11th May 1907, the postcard reads: "Just so that you won't forget what it is like".

Bourneville Girls leaving Cycle House.

GIRLS LEAVING CYCLE HOUSE

The corridors, exits and entrances were so arranged that male and female workers did not meet.
Posted 7th August 1907 the postcard message reads: ''I went to the flower show yesterday with
Russells. It was at Holders. We all went on that little railway, it wasn't half all right''.

THE GREEN

Following the construction of the shops in circa 1906, the Bournville Post Office and the post mistress, Mrs M J Patteson, transferred to the Green from 84 Linden Road. This card is dated circa 1907, and published by O W Evans, The Pharmacy, Bournville.

THE GREEN

Eliza Wetton sold her tobacconist shop to Richard Grant in 1925. By 1928 he had sold the business to Albert Creed. Posted 18th March 1927 the card reads: ''Hope you will have a good meeting tomorrow. Laura sent on a letter containing a dust cap from Mrs Osbourne, and says we can sell it''.

THE GREEN

The shops from left to right are: Honeybourne Bros (butchers), J J Bydon & Son (tailors), F P Davies (glass and china dealer), and finally Lloyds Bank. This card was published by A T Ryberg Ltd, 9 Edgbaston Street; the firm subsequently became Adco Ltd. Their numbering exceeded over 2,000, taking in all of Birmingham.

THE GREEN

It was only fitting that Lloyds Bank, another company owing its origins to Birmingham, should be the only clearing bank on Bournville Green. The bank manager at this time was Albert Harris. This is also an A T Ryberg card.

THE GREEN

A view of the shops on the Green before the Rest House was built. Posted 21st August 1907, the postcard message reads: ''We have been here today, it is a beautiful place. We all went out about 3 o'clock, got back about 8.30 pm, just had tea and supper together''.

THE REST HOUSE

The Rest House has been a central feature of the Green since it was opened in May 1914. It was erected through subscription by the world-wide employees of Cadbury Brothers Ltd, to commemorate the Silver Wedding of George and Elizabeth Cadbury in 1913.

THE REST HOUSE

The Rest House was designed by W A Harvey and H G Hicks and modelled on a late medieval English Butter Market. The interior has stone panels, some depicting events in the history of Bournville.

THE MEETING HOUSE
Looking from the top of the school tower and showing Hazel Road, middle right, which was pedestrianised when this part of the Green was changed following the first world war.

BOURNVILLE SCHOOLS

Looking across Hazel Road to the school and tower; the latter building containing a classroom, library and laboratory. Posted 29th December 1909, the postcard was written in French to someone in Burnley, Lancashire.

THE DAY CONTINUATION COLLEGE

The Day Continuation College was a pioneer institution that grew from classes for young industrial employees started by Cadbury Brothers Ltd in 1913. The postcard is dated 16th May 1931.

E.12. BOURNVILLE CAMP WOODS

CAMP WOODS

This woodland area was near the centre of the village. It was called Stocks Wood: Thomas Stock's heirs selling the land to George Cadbury. Adjacent to the wood was the Bournville Village Estate Nursery, and managed by John Jones during the early years of this century.

MINWORTH GREAVES

Minworth Greaves stood for centuries by the side of the Kingsbury Road between Curdworth and Minworth. It is a good example of the Cruck method of building construction dating back to the 13th century. The building was acquired in 1911 by George Cadbury, re-erected and opened to the public on Founders Day in 1932.

THE OLD MANOR

Selly Manor House photographed in its original setting on Bournbrook Road, Bournbrook, about a mile away from its present site. George Cadbury bought it in 1907, had it dismantled, and removed the building to Bournville. The building was reconstructed by A W Harvey.

SELLY MANOR

Selly Manor was re-erected in Bournville between 1912 and 1916; some deficiencies being made up with contemporary building materials. The middle gable is a fine example of Tudor 'brick-nogging'.

MAPLE ROAD

These houses were built circa 1904. One of the first occupants, Randolph Gumbley, lived at number 35 though he had gone by 1907. The postcard is dated c.1912.

MAPLE ROAD

A Bournville map of 1899 shows Maple Road with just one semi-detached block. By 1905 a significant majority of the houses had been built.

ACACIA ROAD

Acacia Road cuts through Stocks Wood. The low sweeping roof to include the porch, the contrasting roof tiling and the three part lower windows with Palladian echoes are further examples of building varieties found throughout Bournville.

56, ACACIA ROAD
Dated 5th March 1907 and showing 56, Acacia Road, Bournville. This was the home of Frederick James Harmer from 1907 to 1914. A fine cottage construction with a hooped effect above the lower windows and an angled two entrance porch.

WILLOW ROAD
Looking up Willow Road from the apex of the triangle with Willow and Sycamore Roads.
Dated May 1914.

WILLOW ROAD

Most of the roads in the original village are thirteen metres wide and would now be considered too wide for a residential area. In 1898 ten separate housing projects were under construction around the Bournville 'building site' Estate.

ELM ROAD

The roads in the village were all constructed in advance of housing development, a considerable undertaking in those days. A W Harvey, architect was involved in a number of later housing projects in West Bromwich, Calthorpe Estate, Edgbaston and other parts of the country.

ELM ROAD

The houses on the north-east side of the village in Elm, Willow and Laburnum Roads were begun in 1897. On the east side of Elm Road below number 31, was a brick and tile factory owned by William Ward of Northfield which provided house bricks and other building materials for the new houses.

HOLLY GROVE

A few experiments in reducing road costs were tried. Holly Grove completed in 1900, contains a small group of houses fronting a simple 3-metre wide footpath. The main reason for these decorative houses next to the railway line was to arouse interest from the passing passenger traffic.

Corner of Laburnum & Willow Rd BOURNVILLE.

THE CORNER OF LABURNUM AND WILLOW ROADS

A view from the north entrance to the Cadbury Works. The photographer of this picture was Thomas Lewis, Stratford Road, Birmingham; the business continues today under the name of John Whybrow Ltd at the same address.

THE TRIANGLE

A view from the south-western apex of the Laburnam Road Triangle. The gap between the houses on the right of the picture is the drive leading to Bournville Village Trust Maintenance Department. This was originally Five Gates Farm, the track to it becoming Willow Road, prior to it being surrounded by housing.

SYCAMORE ROAD

This fine three-storey block of houses with the stepped chimney arrangement on the house next door, brings us back again to Sycamore Road; once more showing the versatility of design and materials to be found in the pre-1914 housing stock of Bournville Village.

20, SYCAMORE ROAD

Posted 8th July 1907, the postcard message reads: ''This is a picture postcard of our house, I thought you would like one, with love from Brookie, 20 Sycamore Road, Bournville''. From 1908 to 1915 it was the home of Albert Holland. By 1911 Bournville had 910 houses on 138 acres and its population was 4,300.

ST. GEORGE'S COURT
St. George's Court, built in 1923 as accommodation for business and professional women, provided self-contained furnished flats and bed-sitting rooms.

BOURNVILLE VILLAGE STEAM LAUNDRY
Bournville Village Steam Laundry began trading in 1909, the proprietors being Crook & Murphy, with its receiving office in Raddlebarn Road. They had a number of 'agents' around the village; one of the agents was a Mrs Cresswell of 12 Sycamore Road.

WOODBROOKE
In 1881 George Cadbury lived at this house, later moving to the Manor House, Northfield (Bristol Road) in 1894, which remained his home until he died in 1922.

SELLY OAK ROAD

This was in fact Row Heath Lane which is now known as Selly Oak Road. Posted 23rd August 1909, the postcard reads: ''This is the Cadbury place, nearly tried for a situation, it's such a nice place''.

THE BEECHES
In near proximity to the picture on page 109 is The Beeches, built in 1908 by George and Elizabeth Cadbury as a convalescent home for poor children. Postally used 23rd August 1911.

FIRCROFT COLLEGE

Fircroft College was founded in 1909 and accommodated male students who took a one year course in political and industrial history, economics and literature. In common with many public buildings during the first world war, Fircroft and The Beeches were turned over to the authorities and converted into convalescent homes for the thousands of injured men from the battle fronts in France and Belgium.

FIRCOTE COLLEGE BOURNVILLE.

FIRCROFT COLLEGE
Looking down Oak Tree Lane which is older than Bournville itself. Before the arrival of Richard and George Cadbury in 1879, Linden Road was a tree-lined drive leading to Bournbrook Hall. The lane skirted the estate to link up with Oak (Bournville) Lane via Row Heath Lane (Selly Oak Road).

BOURNVILLE YOUTH CLUB

Bournville Youth Club was founded in 1900 and led by J H Whitehouse who later became a Member of Parliament. The principle of the Club was 'a busy boy is a good boy'.

LINDEN ROAD AND POST OFFICE
Advertising was something Cadbury was never slow to exploit, and associating it with the Garden Village of Bournville was a useful means of self promotion. Up to 1905 the advertising policy was planned annually with a London Agency, T.B. Browne Ltd.

GIRLS' GYMNASIUM

In 1905 it was decided to bring advertising in house; the new Advertising Office under the general direction of George Cadbury. The 'Childrens Playground' above was in Laurel Grove; the distinctive half-timbering on the house helping to locate it.

PLAYGROUND AND GIRLS' BATHS

An Advertising Committee was started in March 1910, two of its founding members being George and William Cadbury. The latter's signature providing the cursive script for the Cadbury logo which is still used to this day.

CHILDREN'S PLAYGROUND
The opposite picture shows the 'Playground' used by female employees prior to the opening of the Girls Grounds in 1896. The Girls' Baths were not built until 1905.

"SOME OF THE 6,500 EMPLOYEES"

6,500 employees dates the postcard between 1909 and 1912. The number of employees reached 7,000 in 1914, dropping sharply during the first world war and reaching its pre-war level again in 1925.

ADVERTISING POSTCARD, 1920s

One wonders what the Cadbury Management would have made of Elsie and her furry companion when they came to work at Bournville. The back of the card reads: "See the name CADBURY on every piece of Chocolate". This became their main marketing slogan in the early 1920s.

Elsie's fingers trembled with excitement.

POPULAR POSTERS   No. 21.

"A GLASS AND A HALF OF MILK IN EVERY ½LB"

A Valentine & Sons Ltd postcard from the early 1930s. The 'Glass and a Half of Milk' is Cadbury's longest running advertising logo, first introduced in 1928. Cadbury's Milk Chocolate was introduced in 1897, achieving real success with the public after 1905.